All Those Years Underwater

All Those Years Underwater

Poems by

Jessica Dubey

Cover design by Shay Culligan
Author photo by Emily Bond, Emmy Marie Photography
Cover photo by Pawel Czerwinski for unsplash.com

ISBN: 978-1-63980-224-1

Kelsay Books
502 South 1040 East, A-119
American Fork, Utah 84003
Kelsaybooks.com

For my sisters—
Lisa, Shelly and Lynn

I'd like to express gratitude to my fellow Grapevine Poets whose friendship and talent have greatly enriched my writing life. To all the members of the Boiler House Poets Collective who have helped me pick out my big girl pants and get serious about my writing goals. To the multi-talented Marilyn McCabe who, if you're lucky, is good for a spontaneous cheer or punch in the arm—you never know which—both high praise. To Liz Rosenberg and Suzanne Cleary for making the time to read this book and for their much-appreciated endorsements. To Elizabeth Cohen, a supremely talented writer and champion of other writers. To my dear friend, Judy Goldschmidt, for helping me find order in the disorder. And to my family for their love and support.

Acknowledgments

Many thanks to all the publications that have published the following poems or earlier versions of them.

The American Journal of Poetry: "Obit for My Father"

Barren Magazine: "All Those Years Underwater"

Black Heart Magazine: "My daughter wants to derail trains," "Mutiny," "The Story of Your Birth"

Kissing Dynamite: "The New Math"

Oxidant | Engine: "Body Literature," "Mission Statement"

Rat's Ass Review: "Needle in the Groove"

Shark Reef: "Departure"

Contents

There is no grief like the grief that does not speak.
—Henry Wadsworth Longfellow

We do not remember days, we remember moments.
—Cesare Pavese

All Those Years Underwater

Three p.m. and the gates
        to the neighbors' pool open.
I throw myself into the water,
        chase the burn
of chlorine, the muffled Eden
        at the bottom, so intolerably
beautiful. Fight the urge to breathe,
        float upwards against
my will. Repeat until exhaustion, until
        the dinner cry from across the fence
so thick with forsythia I can't see
        my own home's dark siding.
The neighbors stencil "Praise the Lord"
        on the bottom of the pool before they fill it,
tell us to shout it
        before we jump in and I do,
despite my doubts,
        just for the chance to be submerged.
Later Mom's boyfriend takes us all
        to a pond in the woods.
Tells us we're going skinny dipping.
        Sounds like an ice cream bar.
Who wouldn't want something so sweet?
        We're too young for euphemisms—
too many syllables, too much depth.
        He drives us down a dirt path
to the pond with our suits and towels.
        Our mother shotgun and silent.
He makes us peel away the protective layer
        and walk one by one into the cold water.

My toes search the bottom
      for an escape. Down
where sound warps
      into a soothing whoosh.
Down where I can't hear him insist
      I swim closer.

Body Literature

This is not my sex tape it was not
sex so no record was kept though the exposure
feels like a third degree burn I expect the pain
will last longer than any one
act it has a pattern of grooves so it lives
in long-term memory next to the line
I cut to get to the roller coaster
faster next to the kitten I rescued and named
catastrophe it might last longer
than the memory of the other I
can't be sure of the half-life after
the skin peeled away the jumper cables
latched onto nerve endings the result
was a howl disembodied from the beast this
is the howl reentering the body

Photo of My Father's Fishing Trip, Summer 1970

My father's lips pull back
into a smile, cigarette clenched

in his teeth, a pike as long as his torso
raised for the camera,

mouth agape in astonishment
at being caught as it dangles

from the stringer, one fish
but fish enough

to call this trip a success,
this moment on the edge

of a lake that skims the sky,
the only feature not faded with time,

while the grass and his flannel shirt
begin to dull as soon as the photo

is developed, the tree behind him
losing its embrace

of my father, the landscape for all I know
unrecognizably altered, cleared

for a vacation home
with a wrap-around porch,

a dock that leads to a waiting boat
ready to float a fisherman

through retirement over schools
of fish descended from my father's catch

swimming toward the pull of hooks
and nets, flashing their tails

as they writhe on the floor of the boat
alongside crushed beer cans

and assorted lures, discarded
like the insides of the pike,

the filet knife slitting its belly open
so my father could run

his thumb along each bone
of the spine erasing the stomach,

the liver, the heart, to share
a meal with his buddies, unseen

in the photo, one of whom
captured this moment of pride,

this friend who might have been the one
five years later who turned

his snowmobile around
and raced for help or perhaps

stayed and knelt by my father's side
worrying over the quickly fading daylight.

Needle in the Groove

Here we are again at the confluence
        of hot car seat and kitten
                with a broken neck
I am buckled
        into the same car
                that minutes earlier left
its radial tire imprint
        on my left thigh
                I am buckled
into the same memory
        that imprints on my mind
                and later the kitten
imprinted on the Labrador
        who with its soft gaping love
                picked it up
strode across the lawn
        lapping up the kitten's newness
                its just-opened eyes
took it in its noble mouth
        and rolled it from its tongue
                past awful teeth
to my father's feet
        who scooped up the barely-there
                kitten in one hand
hammer in the other
        and walked out of sight
                I reach back
from the driver's seat
        for the little girl
                road rash on her back
fusing with hot vinyl
        I reach for the kitten
                the loll of its neck

reach for my father's hand
        soft and dangerous
                as the canine mouth
reach and reach and find only
        the splintered handle
                of the hammer

Someone threw a rock at a moving car

and you can't go home   you might as well
            ride your bike   into the oncoming
                    dusk   might as well ride the streets
            hands free   and if you fall and hit your head
even if you puke   there's no sympathy
            and the blood   from your teeth
forcing themselves   into your lower lip   when you land
            tastes of umami   but you don't know
                    that word   though you've heard
some blood is better than others   which proves
            mosquitos don't know shit   because they've been
                    carrying you away   a drop at a time
            all summer   and you want to go home
            but the shop dog   is off its chain
                    and there's only a ten-speed
keeping it from taking   what's left of you
            and the highway   is a line
                    you could cross   but don't
            because her boyfriend's reach is long
and he's lifted you up   and tacked you like a notice
            to the door before   and who's to say
                    it's not a threat   it's a promise
            is just talk   and it will be years   after you leave
before it enters your mind   that he might have done
                    to your sisters   what he's done to you
            but like big words   you don't know that yet
all you know   is that the dark comes from all directions
                    this time of the night   and the mosquitos
                    aren't finished with you yet

Mission Statement

My brother used to sleepwalk
as a child. Mom would find him
out back, pissing off the porch
in the middle of night.
Her ears perked to the creak
of door hinges and footsteps
that could easily have been confused
with anything else,
her brain as it was, flooded with sleep.
She worried he'd wander off
or do something reckless
in his altered state.
Awake he was prone
to his own brand
of Rock 'Em Sock 'Em chaos,
looking for the sweet spot
to knock someone's head off,
piloting fists that pummeled
whatever got in his way.
He broke toys, some unintentionally,
others while trying to pry apart their secrets.
He broke toes, but only his own.
Mostly he broke rules.
For fun, he'd rim the ledge
of his bedroom window
with modeling glue,
strike a match, let it burn.
But asleep, that was when
the edges came off
and all he wanted to do
was put that fire out.

The Story of Your Birth

Let's start with that night.
All can agree the doctor was drunk,
though he died long ago
and cannot dispute the martinis
that cured a day of office visits
and expectant mothers.

Back up a few hours
to the Italian sausage, the heartburn.
Grandma stirred the pot,
then the contractions got rolling.
Let's assume Dad drove fast,
every bump in the road egged you on.

At the hospital, the nurses wheeled Mom
to the room where she waited
for that doctor whose party you interrupted.
There was pain. Some of it might have been yours,
but you don't remember.

At the height of her agony,
Mom rose off the delivery table
trying to leave her body behind.
One nurse held Mom's legs, the other her shoulders.
They pressed her to the table
as if opening a jackknife.

Light tore through her.
Stars gave way to a hypnotic sky.
Enter the doctor, with his antiseptic breath.
Enter you, so pretty, blue as Delft porcelain

Backdraft

I hear a knock at the door
the house I grew up in
struggling to breathe
turn the knob
apple from a branch
of my family
spit up and cigarettes
with the modeling glue
on the windowsill
combusted
like the smell of chlorine
then the punched hole
my brother's fist
the poor patch job
where my sister slept
mute and unable to walk
I hear the pounding
in my chest

find myself outside
face pressed to glass
this place back to life
wrestle an underripe
the scent
peanut butter and dander
melded together
squeezed out
how flame
in my nose
a necessary burn
in the wall
searching
as penance
that cold room
far from mother's room
the beating
the only answer

Mutiny

The house, this morning,
is filled with fog.
I swim through it from my bed
to the kitchen sink
without ever touching
the cold Italian tiles.
Parts of me, still recognizable,
float atop the froth.
I wish for your hand
to reach out, scoop me up
the way a slotted spoon skims fat
from a bubbling broth.
I will stay in this dead man's float
and lap up the hours.
This is only a body,
or what looks like one
when you squint at the clouds
and see a rabbit or a ship.
That's it. I am a ship.
You are the mutiny.

Before We Married

That ordinary clothesline, outstretched,
bears the weight of damp ornaments—
tea towels and blouses, summer sheets
and silky nightgowns—now decked out
with two roses stripped
of their thorny defenses,
two pairs of men's briefs,
not so out of place, though hopefully laundered,
but there to yell, *look here,* in case the roses
fail in their beauty to turn my head,
all of them dangling there in service
of one envelope zipped up in plastic
and held by a single clothespin,
some secret correspondence
and the real star of this show
because days before, under a moonless sky,
he lifted my hood
and jimmied the distributor cap,
loosened it so my engine wouldn't turn,
so it stood there useless
while he waited for the call
begging for his hands
to fix what he had broken,
but I didn't call,
and so now this display
on my grandmother's clothesline
below the window where I sleep
dreaming of what he cannot decipher,
but knowing I can't resist
that envelope, which I take down
but not before I smell
the roses, though most certainly

not the underwear, then open
his letter which includes a sketch
he's made of me, the first hint
of his talent, and a poem,
every word plagiarized
to perfection.

A Litany of Falling Stars

I can see all the way to the Andromeda galaxy
      how it wraps
           & spirals
                around everything
                    it loves
A clutch of moons and suns
      within its gravitational embrace
          as if all
              that swirls in
                & around it
emanates from a single strand
      of DNA
              I see that—

& everything beyond it
      the crash coming
the force of repelling
      & coming back together
              exasperating the laws
              of attraction

I don't know why
      I stay

   In the beginning
      we climbed onto the roof
& thrilled at the burn
      of hot tar on bare thighs

   You spilled a beer on my arm
      offered to lick it off
How could I have known
      you wanted to swallow me whole?

We should have been fishing
from the rooftop   casting lines
                    into the unknown
                              throwing back
        everything
                    that was too small to keep

It was all
                    too small to keep

        When our son feared
the ceiling above his bed opened
                    to the night sky
        I told him
it was all in his imagination
        He said
                    he didn't want one anymore

        In own my imagination
                    I displace
            all the spent rockets
                    all the celestial bodies
            the satellites
                        that have lost their bearings
        I become   unmistakable

My daughter wants to derail trains

and rip off the neighbors.
She wants to sell firecrackers to 8-year-olds
and throw rocks at windows.
The stories of her father's childhood

hum through her veins.
She wants to eat mischief
for breakfast,
let it spill on the floor

so the ants can join the anarchy.
I tried to raise her up to accept pigtails and polish.
She wants sticks and stones and stories
to tell her own children.

At night she begs her father
for one more bedtime tale.
She envisions him
Peter Pan meets Marvel superhero

with a bad boy twist.
She knows these stories
call to her from another time.
They're ones she could never quite recreate

without getting caught.
But in her wildest dreams,
when no one is looking,
that's exactly what she does.

The New Math

I couldn't help   my children

with the new   math   all those

          unfamiliar
                    steps
                              to get
                              to the same   answer

          Such fussiness   with   remainders
          teaching them how to carry   over

                              Now   all those

          new   children
who   go   to school

          steep   learning curves
                    weighing them

                              down
                              like Kevlar   backpacks
All those ballistic   lessons   they have to commit

          to memory   The active killer   kits

with tourniquets   they have to   turn   turn   turn

          to stop the loss   The choices
                    they have   to make   how to be

battlefield   ready   and what to do
          with all those   remainders

30

Departure

In my daughter's dream
     I reach   for the saltshaker
        Parts of me
          dis-
              solve
        I dab the corners
   of my mouth
       The napkin
            falls
  from a hand
       no longer there
   I am dust
       circling a dream
sifting
     through my own remains
       for someone else's symbolism—
    wishbone
  heart charm
      luggage tags
    My daughter speed-reads
      every omen
  tattoos them
      between her fingers
    in white ink
       only I can read
    I pour
her morning mantra
    add extra milk
       She sees
         clouds
    stirs them up
  Let them be
    I tell her
   I cannot fly
     through so much   turbulence

Love &

We collect   anniversaries   let them

          pile up   with the furniture   photographs

                    our half-spent affections

He buys flowers   I start a love poem

     write instead   about a slick road   failings

               of the thin tread   of our worn skin

               how we
                         slip
                              & slip
                              repeating   our history

Listen   I know   what love is

          what it does

                         & doesn't

     This was never going to be   a sonnet

Every word   honed

          into weaponry   forged

                    for each reckless cut

Then silence   a slow death

It's not   that passion

wasn't a knife   It's just

that the blade wanted   sharpening

How to Go On—An Erasure

An erasure of Joan Didion's The Year of Magical Thinking, *chapters 1 & 2*

i.

Words change
nothing

Unremarkable errand
in flames

They have no living blood
to convey blood

Where an idea ends
words collapse

ii.

Build the house
Build fires
Don't mix them

iii.

Scrub time away
a mote of minutes

Plot the brain
misremembering silence

It's okay

Watch the still wind
break down

iv.

Discuss minefield
of resentments

v.

Insist the night
split open
a season of bruises

A void left in its place
artificial pearls

vi.

Board the door
a game
where the point
is difficult to declare

Just play

vii.

Write that night
into a running fever

viii.

Spend a wish

Count out how much grief
it dislodges

A depth charge
of magical thinking

Obit for My Father

Thomas J. Shearer died on January 8, 1975, though he's been seen, hedge trimmers in hand, sprucing the shrubs of an elderly neighbor. The neighbor died in 1963, which proves nothing at all. In high school he made the varsity wrestling team. Though he was athletic, flat feet and thick glasses kept him from serving our country. His mother says his letter sweater is full of moth holes, which proves nothing at all. Rumor has it he's been spotted marching with a gas can through an open field of snow toward a stalled snowmobile. Witnesses say he was difficult to see as the whiteness nearly blotted him out and, from a distance, he looked like a single period punctuating the page. The author of this obituary prefers to think of him as an ellipsis . . . A Polaroid of him on his wedding day in 1965 shows him in perfect health. He has not appeared in a photograph since 1975, which proves nothing at all. In 1987, he became a grandfather. He has since welcomed eleven more grandchildren into the family. He has never met any of them, which proves nothing at all.

Family Donates Snowmobile After Father's Fatal Accident, January 1975

That January squall
    stripped everything down
        a collage of white on white

        I peered outside
           at the erasure
A knoll stood
    like something hushed
        in the making

So many times
    I climbed that hill
    looked out
        into the woods
toward the glen
    where our aging Labrador
    crept off
        didn't return

    Summers
    the knoll
        a bay of quivering green
my fingers combing
    baby mice from its
        strands

I held their squirming
    naked
        blindness

Cried when dad pushed
    the lawnmower
        up one side of that hill

    down the unseeable
    other side

If nearly every cell in the body is replaced every seven years

I'm going to forget him one day.
As it is, I'm down to the last sliver
of him. By the end of the week
he could be the gap
between two teeth or a healed
paper cut. I'll have to strip a rib
of rebar from my chest to pry him loose
or squint to see the gone shadow
of him, though squinting
is a form of forgetting too,
a pillow that smothers the periphery.
All you have to do is let your lids find
each other, let that one thing
or that one person be starved of light
and they're gone.
When I was 8-years-old, I was stuffed
into a clothes hamper by an older child
who sat on the lid and refused to move.
My body folded like dirty laundry.
No air, no light. A moment longer
and I would have forgotten
myself. How is it that I remember
that day but I am forgetting him?
Ever since, I've felt the slow cascade
of time cells, with him as their nucleus,
being swept away. And the brain,
like a fat baby in its fetal position,
does nothing to stop it.

I'm in the process of going extinct

My greatest wish
        is to be remnant

If my finger bones are all
             that's left for sequencing
      let them be my pinkies

Tell the person who finds them
         they were warmed
               at the hearth
        of other bodies

      that I tangoed
with postmodern man
        and our offspring decoded
             the language of trees

        As I go
I promise to leave   pieces of me
        in all the places I've ever visited

        —the beveled basin of my pelvis
        tucked into the Amazon

my breastbone split
       between Tunisia   and Timbuktu—

         to give anthropologists
         restless nights
            dreaming

of origins

If possible
I'd like to be found
under a seabed

the waves in concert
my two little fingers   conducting the search

About the Author

Jessica Dubey is a poet living in Endicott, NY. She is a member of the Boiler House Poets Collective which convenes annually for a poetry residency at The Studios of the Massachusetts Museum of Contemporary Art. She has been nominated for a Best of the Net and her work has appeared in numerous journals including *Oxidant | Engine, Barren Magazine, Gulf Stream Literary Magazine, The American Journal of Poetry,* and *Kissing Dynamite.* Her first chapbook, *For Dear Life,* was published in May 2022.

www.ingramcontent.com/pod-product-compliance
Lightning Source LLC
Chambersburg PA
CBHW031009090426
42737CB00008B/740